Aloha!
Martin Titz
200?

Hawaiian Lotus / Heather L.Titus
P.O. Box 3630
Lihue, HI 96766

hawaiianlotus.com

Hawaiian Principles of Living by Kahu Abraham Kawai'i, Kahuna ©

Hawaiian Principles of Living Ho'okahi Ho'oulu Kawai'i ©

Universal Principles of Living Amrit Yoga Institute ©

Hawaiian Poetical Sayings by Mary Kawena Pukui

Photography by Heather Titus ©

Contributing photographers:

G. Brad Lewis ©

Douglas Peebles ©

Steven Whitsell ©

ISBN # 978-0-9762351-2-5   Hard Cover
ISBN # 978-0-9762351-3-2   Soft Cover

Library of Congress catalog card number #1-621124-1
PRE000000667

First printing of this edition 2007
Printed in China

Na Pua O'lohe

HO'OKAHI HO'OULU KAWAI'I

WRITING & EDITING

Hawaiian Lotus

P H O T O G R A P H Y

HEATHER TITUS

PHOTOGRAPHER

DESIGN / LAYOUT

TEXT COMPILATION

COVER DESIGN

CONTRIBUTING PHOTOGRAPHERS:

Volcano Images

G. BRAD LEWIS

DOUGLAS PEEBLES

Hawaii- A State of Being

Aloha.

I send forth my breath with you.

A journey of compassion.

...he ancient art of navigation begins with the voyage upon the seas of the inner mind.

Kahu Abraham Kawai'i, Kahuna

"In the breath of a moment existences are formed and transformed.
Worlds within worlds, lives within lives... The expanded self transcends the eternities... There is no time..."

Within these pages Kahuna Abraham Kawai'i illuminates ancient Hawaiian kahuna principles of living
that are universal in nature. Ancient cultures throughout the world express these principles in different ways;
although differing in modalities and symbols, their essence remains the same.

Universal principles provide a path to access our birthright to wholeness ~
wholeness that can be applied to all aspects of our lives.

The direction of this book was initiated by Kahu Abraham Kawai'i, Kahuna.
He founded Na Pua 'Olohe, the school where his teachings continue to this day. Here the Ancient Hawaiian
Kahuna principles of living are interwoven to reflect the spiritual values of the ancient culture. These values are just as true today.

Ho'okahi Ho'oulu ,the wife and longtime student of Kahu Abraham Kawai'i
plays the important role of teacher and interpreter of his work. She continues to teach in Hawai'i and throughout the world.

This book is dedicate to...

Kahu Abraham Kawai'i, Kahuna

Kamini Desai

Ho'okahi Ho'oulu Kawai'i

Beyond the horizon of evolution.

Touched by greatness, all greatness is accessed.

Kahu Abraham Kawaiʻi, Kahuna

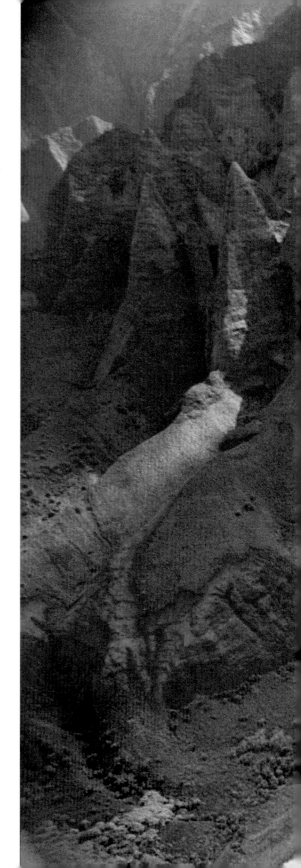

Na Pali, Kauai

'Onipa'a.

Fixed, steadfast, forever... In love and dignity

Kailua, Oahu

10

I stand upon a mountain

which stands upon an island

which lies upon an ocean

which is upon a planet

which is within a universe

which is - I.

Ones gaze to the glistening stars and the horizon of life expands.

Ma keia ʻaina e pulama

mai i loko o kuʻu na ʻau.

The land which has nurtured me

in its depths fills my heart.

Waiʻaleʻale, Kauai

The breeze brings life to spirit…
infinite rhythms celebrating existence.

Ho'okahi Ho'oulu Kawai'i

Kapa'a, Kauai

As the moon reflects the sunlight
The mind reflects the soul.

Ho'okahi Ho'oulu Kawai'i

Aligning breath

with the rhythm of nature

aligns the heart.

Hoʻokahi Hoʻoulu Kawaiʻi

I am that which I seek.

Kahu Abraham Kawai'i, Kahuna

Carried within the grace and ease of the flow.

I hoʻokahi kahi ke aloha.

Be one in love

Be united in bonds of affection

26

The harmony of nature is found in the impersonal.

Kahu Abraham Kawai'i, Kahuna

A sanctuary ... Lawai Valley

How we take life is how life takes us.

Kahu Abraham Kawai'i, Kahuna

Waimea Canyon, Kauai

Ka lama ku o ka noʻeau

standing torch of wisdom.

To see expanses is to be in motion.

To be in motion changes consciousness.

Kahu Abraham Kawai'i, Kahuna

Puʻukoholā Heiau

Compassion embraces the light and the dark.

Ho'okahi Ho'oulu Kawai'i

Repetition with awareness refines one's skills.

Hoʻokahi Hoʻoulu Kawaiʻi

The greatest state is to dance with eternities.

The challenges of life are food for the soul.

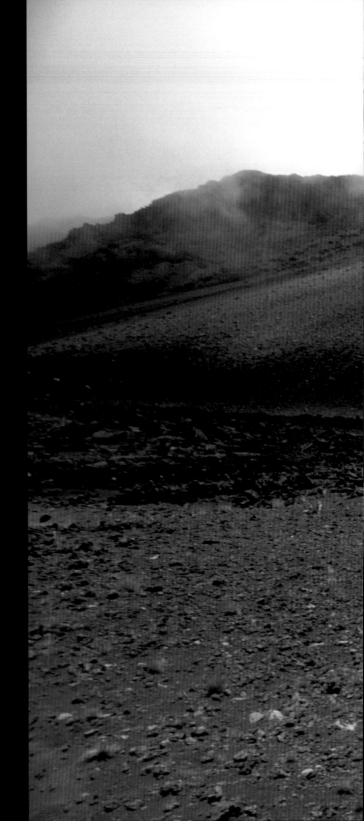

is to maintain the unknown–

is to be in reality.

Kahu Abraham Kawai'i, Kahuna

Haleakala, Maui

There is no experience independent of the meaning you give to it.

Mauna Kea, The island of Hawaii

Life is not measured by the number of breaths you take,

but by the moments that take your breath away.

Kahu Abraham Kawai'i, Kahuna

Waves rise and fall within the ocean,
though the ocean remains the same.

Sunset Beach, Oahu

Each moment is a living prayer.

Kahu Abraham Kawai'i, Kahuna

Having no expectations allows life to be all that it can be.

Carried by the breath into the expanses,
beauty will move within you forever.

Ho'okahi Ho'oulu Kawai"i

54

Mauí

Expand the range of your vision.

Expand the range of your heart.

Hoʻokahi Hoʻoulu Kawaiʻi

Waimanalo, Oahu

I am in the stars above,

I am in the grains of sand on the beaches,

I am in the seas that meet the shores,

I am in the clouds,

I am in the wind,

I am within you,

I am in your next breath,

I am around you .

I am I

Kahu Abraham Kawai'i, Kahuna

Lanikai, Oahu

Opening to the vastness of that which I am.

Ho'okahi Ho'oulu Kawai'i

Vision.
   Seeing what is coming so that you may meet it.

                              Kahu Abraham Kawai'i, Kahuna

Kaneohe, Oahu

Be content with what you have.

Refine it!

It is the starting point.

Kahu Abraham Kawai'i, Kahuna

Kaneohe, Oahu

Action is life's dance.
Hesitation puts the breaks on.

Hoʻokahi Hoʻokahi Kawaiʻi

The calm, clear mind
penetrates the veils effortlessly.

Makena Beach, Maui

Life is about who you are—

not what you do.

Hoʻokahi ka ʻilau like ana.

Wield the paddles together.

Work together.

He ʻonipaʻa ka ʻoiaʻiʻo.

Truth is not changeable

Truth is truth

There is only the substance of truth

It is.

Kahu Abraham Kawaʻi, Kahuna

The Academy of Hawaiian Arts

O ke aloha ke kuleana o kahi malihini.

Compassion makes its home in any land.

Kailua, Oahu

E waikahi ka pono i manalo.

It is well to be united in thought

That all may have peace.

Lean into that which you resist

and your horizon will expand.

Kahu Abraham Kawai'i, Kahuna

The expanse of the Iwas' wings glide gracefully across the horizon.

The fabric of life is arranged through the quality of our thoughts.

Mind follows breath...
Breath flows into relaxation.

On the road to Hana, Maui

I am the giver
I am the receiver
I am that which is given

Kahu Abraham Kawai'i, Kahuna

Ho'omaka i ka 'onohi o ka la.

Beauty appears with the rising sun.

Judgments of others are a reflection of one's own image and likeness.

———

Hanalei Pier, Kauai

'Au i ke kai me he manu ala.

Cross the sea as a bird.

The path of the bird shows the endless sea.

Nothing is taken away.

All is given to those who see.

Ho'okahi Ho'oulu Kawai'i

Ancient Salt Ponds, Kauai

u we ka lani, ola ka honua.

when the sky weeps, the earth revives.

Freedom is your ability to choose a response to any given situation.

O na hoku no ke kauaheahe o ka lani.

The heavenly gaze is upon us.

I am complete unto myself.
Infinite starlight glistening
in the ecstasy of self.

Contentment.

Life comes as a wave

... Catch the wave.

Waimea Beach, Oahu

Flow is how the universe communicates with you.

Kahu Abraham Kawai'i, Kahuna

With compassion everything becomes family.

Kahu Abraham Kawai'i, Kahuna

I ka ʻolelo no ke ola; I ka ʻolelo no ka make.

Life within speech; Death within speech.

The eyes also speak.

Drink from the inner spring of joy.

Wailua Falls, Kauai

The source of love lies within…

within the stillness,

silence penetrates the expanses of our being containing eternities.

Po'ipu, Kauai

It is not about opposites – it is about oneness.

Haleakala Crater, Maui

Change an opinion and in one moment –

you have changed your life.

Kahu Abraham Kawai'i, Kahuna

Freedom lies within commitment.

Fill yourself with silence…
The ecstasy of the eternal self.

Hoʻokahi Hoʻoulu Kawaiʻi

I am the performer

I am the performance

I am that which is preformed

Kahu Abraham Kawai'i, Kahuna

Noho i ka pono a ʻike ʻia mai e na akua.

Continue to live righteously until the Gods recognize you.

Conquer fear with compassion.

Hoʻokahi Hoʻoulu Kawaiʻi

The divine creator exists behind and within all.

Kahu Abraham Kawai'i, Kahuna

In the wonderment is the mystery of life.

Hoʻolike ka manaʻo i wailohi.

Open to the brilliance of what is.

When you acknowledge life,

Life will acknowledge you.

Kahu Abraham Kawai'i, Kahuna

Makua Beach, Kauai

The body contains the spirit,
motion unites spirit with nature.

Hoʻokahi Hoʻoulu Kawaiʻi

Soft sands are formed out of the roughest seas.

Kahu Abraham Kawai'i, Kahuna

Secret Beach, Kauai

A'ohe mea 'imi a ka maka.

Nothing more for the eyes to search for.

Everything desired is in your presence.

Lumaha'i Beach, Kauai

O ka mea ua hala ua hala ua.

In the heart of forgiveness everything becomes family.

wai o kaunu.

waters of love.

The thrilling effects of being in love.

On the road to Hana, Maui

ke Kahiau

One who gives lavishly and generously from the heart expecting nothing in return.

On the road to Hana, Maui

Stars come, stars go

Moon rises, moon sets

Sands shift beneath my feet

I am the "I" that sees.

Kahu Abraham Kawai'i, Kahuna

Self fulfillment needs no validation.

Kailua Beach, Oahu

ka ʻoli me ke e uwalo i ka laʻi

My joy resounds in this existence.

In the depths of dignity lies the true self.

Kahu Abraham Kawai'i, Kahuna

Me he lau no ke Ko'olau ke oloha.

Love is elusive, like the breeze of the Ko'olaus.

Ko'olau, Kaneohe

Now is a reality-
built on the past with dreams of the future.

Ho'okahi Ho'oulu Kawai'i

Waikiki, Oahu

In reality "should have" and "could have" do not exist.

Kahu Abraham Kawai'i, Kahuna

ka ipukukui pio 'ole i ke kaua'ula

...The light that will not go out in spite of

the blowing of the Kaua'ula wind.

...The passionate heart does not flee before

the strong winds.

Ka la ʻi o hauola

Peace and contentment

Lanikai, Oahu

He ʻolina leo ka ke aloha.

Joyousness within the voice of love.

The secret message between the words brings me a sweet joy.

Ola i ka wai a ka ʻopua.

The clouds contain the waters of life.

Say yes to what is and nothing can hurt you.

Kahu Abraham Kawaiʻi, Kahuna

Hanalei, Kauai

Peace is found by the one that watches.

Kailua Beach, Oahu

The fewer the expectations –
The freer you are to be.

Halau Hula Pua Ali'i

Ua mau ke ea o ka ʻaina i ka pono.

The land is perpetuated in righteousness.

Kalalau Beach, Kauai

Ka ua 'o'ili'ili maka akua.

The fine, sprinkling of rain denotes the presence of the gods.

The experience of fulfillment is not a result of what you have or do not have.

ka ulua kapapa oke kai loa

The power of the ulua fish of the deep sea

A passionate longing as deep as the heart

Ke e Beach, Kauai

Ka makani hali ʻana i ke ala onaona.

The fragrance-bearing breeze...

it's so intoxicating.

Kalalau, Koke'e State Park, Kauai

A'ohe loa i ka hana a ke aloha.

Distance is ignored by love.

Alekoko
Menehune Fish Pond, Kauai

174

Cherish the 'aina and it will give back to you.

Plant the seeds of thought in the past and the
future and you do not plant in the now.
You reap no harvest.

Ho'okahi Ho'oulu Kawai'i

Taro Fields, Hanalei, Kauai

No kahí ka pílíkía, pau a pau.

when you honor your troubles as a prayer

They come to an end.

waipahe wale.

Gentle as still water

A person who is gentle and kind.

The simplicity of now gives life to peace within.

He poʻi na kai uli, kai koʻo, ʻaʻohe hina pukoʻa.

Though the sea be deep and rough, the coral remains standing.

One who remains calm in the face of difficulty.

He punawai kahe wale ko kakou aloha.

Love is a spring that flows freely.

Love without bounds ... it exists for all.

Waikani Falls,
on the road to Hana, Maui

Lana kakou i ka hauʻoli o haʻi

We rise by uplifting others.

Ola i ke ahe lau makani.

The life within the gentle breath of the breeze

Flow ...align yourself with it.

Ho'eu eu ka 'aina ia loko.

The essence of the 'aina brings a deep stirring within my being.

Ke'e Beach, Kauai

In the simplicity of the smallest movement great change occurs.

Ke lele o ka lani.

Flight of the heavenly one.

Na Pali, Kauai

Love never fails - expectations do.

The universe exists in balance
Balance in every motion of nature.

Opaeka'a Water Falls, Kauai

Enjoy the ride, for change is inevitable.

Jaws, Maui

Kupanaha au i ke ola o ke ahiahi.

The sounds in the evening bring endless fascination.

Kalalau, Koke'e State Park, Kauai

Reach for it and it moves away.
      relax… breathe…   it comes to you.

Kahu Abraham Kawai'i, Kahuna

Waimea Beach, Oahu

He ʻohu ke aloha; ʻaʻohe kuahiwi kau ʻole.

Love is like the mist:

there is no mountaintop it does not settle upon.

Love comes to all.

Kahiko o ke akua.

The adornment of the gods

A shower of rain—
the gods express their approval.

Waimea Canyon, Kauai

He po walea, he ao walea i ka la'i.

Presence brings serenity

Halau Hula 'Pua Ali'i

The petals of love form as a lei within my heart

He waiwai nui ka lokahi.

Unity is the most precious possession.

Love and dignity are the highest. They want nothing.

Kahu Abraham Kawai'i, Kahuna

Halau Mohala 'Ilima

215

ua ola loko i ke aloha.

Love gives life within.

Alekoko
Menehune Fish Pond

You love that in yourself which is awakened by the other.

Relax… take a breath… don't take yourself so seriously.

A'ohe hana nui ke alu 'ia.

No task is too big when shared by all.

Let your breath carry you.

Being in dignity is expansive and maintains you.

Halau Hula Olana

Perpetuate dignity by being one with your environment...

Kahu Abraham Kawai'i, Kahuna

Na Pali, Kauai

Ku ka honu i ka malie.

The turtle poised quietly.

Gracefully at ease with the world.

Kailua Beach, Oahu

There are no mistakes in life-
Only choices and consequences

Ho'okahi Ho'oulu Kawai'i

231

Achieve in a lifetime, a year, a day...

life is motion.

The timing is up to you.

Kahu Abraham Kawai'i, Kahuna

Koke'e State Park, Kauai

Wai aku i ka lani.

Let the selecting take place in heaven.

Choose the path of what is ... and you choose the path of heaven.

234

Eternal Rhythms

Be ....Take a breath and step across the line.

Kahu Abraham Kawai'i, Kahuna

Continuous movement - say yes!

It is the continuum of motion.

Kahu Abraham Kawai'i, Kahuna

Ecstasy fills the eternal dance of life.

Halau Hula Olana

Internal harmony reflects in the world around us.

Kahu Abraham Kawai'i, Kahuna

Be the dance.

Hula Halau 'O Kamuela

What one focuses on, one gives life to.

Kahu Abraham Kawai'i, Kahuna

The present holds hands with the past and the future.

244

Aia ka wa'a i ka iwi Hilo o Hawaii.

The canoe lies at the heart of the Hawaiian culture.

Placement is deliberate, it achieves results.

Kahu Abraham Kawai'i, Kahuna

... Evolving the past forward

Poli'ahu Heiau, Kauai

Ko ke kahuna ha'i kupua.

the kahuna belongs the duty of declaring the revelations of the supernatural beings

Hauola Heiau, Kauai

Dew of Life

He hoʻike na ka po

A revelation of the night

A revelation of the gods in dreams, visions, and omens

valea a ku'ono' ono.

...and make it deep.

Iao Valley, Maui

The rainbow – the gods' promise

Beyond the horizon of evolution.

Kahu Abraham Kawai'i, Kahuna

RESOURCES

HAWAIIAN SPIRITUAL PRINCIPLES OF LIVING
KAHU ABRAHAM KAWAI'I, KAHUNA
HO'OKAHI HO'OULU KAWAI'I
WWW.NAPUAOLOHE.COM

UNIVERSAL SPIRITUAL PRINCIPLES OF LIVING
GURUDEV SHRI AMRITJI AND AMRIT YOGA
WWW.AMRITKALA.COM

'OLELO NO'EAU
HAWAIIAN PROVERBS AND POETICAL SAYINGS
BY MARY KAWENA PUKUI

WRITING & EDITING
FAYE KAWAIILANI HOPE KUMU STEPHENS
WWW.NAPUAOLOHE.COM

PHOTOGRAPHY
HEATHER TITUS / HAWAIIAN LOTUS
WWW.HAWAIIANLOTUS.COM

CONTRIBUTING PHOTOGRAPHERS
VOLCANO IMAGES
G. BRAD LEWIS
WWW.VOLCANOMAN.COM

DOUGLAS PEEBLES
WWW.DOUGLASPEEBLES.COM

STEPHEN WHITESELL
WINDSURFING IMAGE
ROBBIE NAISH

HAWAIIAN TRANSLATIONS
UNIVERSITY PROFESSOR-RETIRED
EMILY HAWKINS

GERMAN TRANSLATIONS
DAVID IPPEN
WWW.NAPUAOLOHE.COM

ACKNOWLEDGEMENTS

"Kumu Mark Keali'i Ho'omalu & The Academy of Hawaiian Arts"

Kumu Hula Kulev Triniдud.Hulu Hulau Kulevvlukuikuhikinuwkulu

Kumu Victoria Holt Takamini, Halau Hula Pua Ali'i

Kumu Olana and Howard Ai, Halau Hula Olana

Kumu Mapuana de Silva, Halau Mohala 'Ilima

Kumu Kaui Kamanao Hula Halau 'O Kamuela

Hula Dancers
Pono Fernandez & Kilihune Kaaihue

Special Thank you:
Na Pua 'Olohe

www.napuaolohe.com

Lawai Center
www.lawaicenter.org

Heritage Graphics Inc.
Richard Lyday

Pacific Whale Foundation
www.pacificwhale.org

Whale Trust
www.whaletrust.org

About the Author

Heather Titus moved from Illinois to Oahu in 1982 where she studied Commercial Art
at Honolulu Community College. She continued her studies of Fine Arts at
Windward Community College for a total of 4 years.

With the unending source of inspiration that is Hawaii surrounding her, she began cultivating
her sight through the medium of photography. By the mid 90's, Ms. Titus gained recognition in
the community for her inspired and exquisite pictures of nature.

Heather Titus' dedication is made clear in the ever-evolving refinement of her photographs.
The unique visions captured on film have opened many avenues for Ms. Titus.
She expresses her mastery of the art in different arenas:
portraiture, prints for home and office decor, a product line of images
on CD and DVD, and stock images of people and nature
which are internationally recognized for their beauty and vision .

To reveal Hawai'i's true essence in photography requires patience and surrender in the artist:
nature is unpredictable, timing is essential.
The flawless moment emerges when light and subject embrace in complete harmony.

"Photographing nature has taught me that life, like light, changes from moment to moment.
Many pictures are fleeting- received in a breath of light that comes into existence and fades,
never to be seen in the same way again."
Heather Titus